Nuncle Music

GARETH REEVES studied at the University of Oxford and at Stanford University, where he held a Wallace Stegner Writing Fellowship. Until recently he was Reader in English at Durham University, where he ran an MA creative writing course in poetry. Carcanet Press have published three previous collections of his poetry. He has also published two books on T.S. Eliot, a book on the poetry of the 1930s (co-authored with Michael O'Neill), and many essays on nineteenth- and twentieth-century English, Irish and American poetry.

BARRIE ORMSBY studied at the Ruskin School of Art (1963–66) and has worked from the landscape of west Durham for the past thirty-five years. He is also a muralist, and founder member of the Bearpark Artists Co-operative.

Also by Gareth Reeves from Carcanet Press

Real Stories
Listening In
To Hell with Paradise: New and Selected Poems

GARETH REEVES

Nuncle Music

Working drawings by Barrie Ormsby

CARCANET

Acknowledgements

A selection of poems from this sequence, some in earlier versions, appeared in my *To Hell with Paradise: New and Selected Poems* (Carcanet, 2012). Grateful acknowledgement is made to the editor of *New Walk*, in which 'Devils, enemies of the people' and an earlier version of '*Thank you, everything is fine*' first appeared; and to the editor of *PN Review*, in which the following poems first appeared: 'Wind-up people, we are all wound up'; 'No toadstools?', 'Dim-witted workers of the "punitive organs"', 'An improvised life, what is that?', and '*Genius and villainy are compatible*'.

First published in Great Britain in 2013 by
Carcanet Press Limited
Alliance House
Cross Street
Manchester M2 7AQ

www.carcanet.co.uk

A CIP catalogue record for this book is available from the British Library

ISBN 978 1 84777 153 7

The publisher acknowledges financial assistance from Arts Council England

Typeset by XL Publishing Services, Exmouth
Printed and bound in England by SRP Ltd, Exeter

Contents

A sequence of monologues 'spoken' from beyond the grave by the Russian composer Dmitri Shostakovich. Hindsight, self-justification, guilt, and the tricks of memory all play their part in the psycho-drama. The sequence reflects 'the Shostakovich wars' that have raged ever since the composer's death in 1975. Was he a dissident or a dissembler? Were his the politics of conformity, resistance, or survival – or a tense, ultimately inscrutable, tangle of all these?

One of Shostakovich's favourite Shakespearean characters was Lear's Fool, who speaks unpalatable truths and calls the king 'nuncle'. Shostakovich's king was Stalin. Hence the title *Nuncle Music*.

♦♦

Revolution is the getting
of a different set of noses
into the trough, with a few idealistic
outriders to lend authenticity.

Composition is the getting
of a different set of noises
into the air, with a few hedonistic
flourishes to fend off authority.

♦♦

Listen, I give you sound.

Make it yours, the whole gamut,
guts fondled and scraped,
squeals, welts, efflorescences,

salves and lacerations, wrenches, jerks,
twists, whines, spidery attenuations,
tensings and relaxations, snarls, snaps,

writhings, retentions, releases,
retchings, brittle disintegrations,
acidities, grips and gripes, floatings,

slidings, slitherings, ironies,
pulsations, inscrutable insinuations,
amplitudes, harmonics, sardonics,

twitchy, spiky, gimletty, gritty, grabby,
fidgety, weepy, grumpy, strung out,
composed in a rush, overwritten,
underwritten, tender, remote, close to –

and the dips
suddenly over the edge like

falling awake in the dark.
Quicksilver,

untranslatable.
Alive at any rate,
at any rate not dead.

This isn't music this is electricity,
eat it you must eat it
every demi-semi-quaver of it.

I follow the labyrinth
into the muddle,

I see a boy
sabred to death by a Cossack,

I hear my art
cut to shreds by the deaf.

◆◆

I said I went to the Finland Station,
I said I knew a dictator was turning up.

Memory scrambles and repeats,
the mind goes round in mad loops,

lost mood music of the soul in limbo
searching for its alter ego

among the new and the familiar
faceless ones, the brass-faced lackeys,

performs its private opera
– triumph, jealousy, failure, fear –

sings, frowns, howls, then turns
in on itself and closes down.

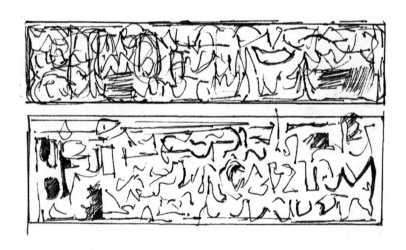

◆◆

The future, it will blow over,
but who put the stars there?

The withering away of illusions takes forever,
like rotting teeth.

But you can pull out a tooth.

This ache becomes me,
I don't know when it started
or if it will stop with me.

They say not to be wise after the event.
But there is no after,

I am the event,
it goes on inside my head
still, over and over.

I shadow-box with myself:

let's have no more patented saviours,
no Stalins, no Solzhenitsyns,

and no more me.

♦♦

Muddle Instead of Music,

six hundred words
scorched on the brain:

shrieking not singing, quacking,
hooting, growling, grunting, gasping,
neurotic, spasmodic, convulsive, fidgety,
primitive, vulgar, coarse, naturalistic,
rutting, crudity, wildness, merchant lust,

death from poisoning and flogging,
tickling perverted tastes of the bourgeoisie,
formalist attempts at originality,
cheap clowning, games of ingenuity,

inside-out leftist muddle.

I turned up late.
A leap year, the usual bad luck.
Why were the brass and percussion so loud?
In the interval the sweaty conductor changed shirts.
Stalin and his cronies shuddered and laughed
and left early.

That did for me:
my unadulterated cacophony,
my pornophony,
my *Lady Macbeth of Mtsensk,*
crucified on the staves.

The martyred Katerina was my Nina,
a genius in her passion:
love is the greatest gift,
and she murdered for love.

Surely our Lover of Euphony,

our Music Critic of Exquisite Taste,
should have warmed to that.
His murders were cold-blooded.

These games could end very badly.

But even if they chop off both my hands
I'll hold the pen between my teeth
and go on writing.

◆◆

These guts churn. The world goes out of focus.
A voice in the dawn queue says *pissed already*.

I don't read *Pravda* for the truth,
I read it for what is being said.

Fear is when you open the paper and it says
you are an enemy of the people.

You look round: people, the people, are reading it,
they whisper, they look at you.

Then they look away.
Silence.

Everything is decided,
you are a non-person,

you are seen through,
you are invisible at last.

Now fear is what you are,
it becomes you.

◆◆

Wind-up people, we are all wound up,
they wind me up, I wind you up.

This is the sharps and flats purge,
now I take it instructions will be given.

As instructed I restructure myself,
I confess to everything and more,
I confirm I conform.

My conformity is contempt.

Listen, I whip myself up in mad
whipping-top white-note noise

– wound-up, whipping, whipped...

and the whipped-up whisperers,
they cross the street,
they cross toward me,

they cross to the other side.

Listen: wound up, whipped up, wiped out,
wiped up, washed out, washed up
among the whispers.

Listen all night by the lift
for car-swish, stair-creak,
door-whisper, the muted rap.

Unpersoned. By whisperers.

◆◆

The circus is pure art,
it can't be forged.
To enter the lion's cage
you can't pull strings,
and try faking the trapeze.

Competing noises, competing voices,
and one buried so deep you cannot hear it.
Music is life, and it is abstract.

Blood running in the street –
make it abstract, make it
audible to the man in the street,

seething and sighing and straining,
through music, through imageless
storyless sound that says nothing,

nothing at all, absolutely
nothing you can hang anything on,
that does not say anything

except the whole bang shoot.

That way the Ox is foxed.

♦♦

Hamlet farts through a flute,
I fart through Hamlet.

Everybody farts
through somebody else,
and the Great Ox farts
through everybody.

Harness slow, ride fast.
Think slow, write fast.

They play me so hard
I can't keep up.

Musical antics.
They wanted to beat us.

Listen, two and two make five
because they say so

and you say it after them
and I say it after you
and my music says it after me
and everyone says it after my music

and I know it's all lies
and you know it's all lies
and they know it's all lies
and everyone knows it's all lies

and my music knows that too.

I fart through my music,
I fart through art.

◆◆

No toadstools?
Then no mushrooms.
Which am I?

In the Big House
the interrogator
shakes my memory:

*Tell us what you know
about the plot to kill Him.*
I don't like gossip.

*Return the day after tomorrow
and you will without fail
remember everything.*

For two nights and a day
I shake:

I shall remember nothing
and go to the Gulag,
I shall remember something
and go to the Gulag,
I shall remember everything
and go to the Gulag.

On the way to the Gulag
I shall lose my nails at least.
Dream of a keyboard
flooding with blood.

The day after tomorrow
my interrogator
has disappeared.

He will lose his nails
at least.

My music is somewhere else,
it has nothing to do with this,

neither toadstool
nor mushroom,
you cannot smell it,
you cannot eat it,

though to say
you cannot die of it
would be a lie.

Hear the monkey's ominous cry.

◆◆

An anthem, do me an anthem,
a contest for a real Russian anthem,
proclaims the Grand Panjandrum.

We all churn away.
Khachaturian and I are instructed
combine your anthems.
I lead him from the path of righteousness,
I pour vodka after vodka,

and hey presto we concoct a
single marvel of art,
a wondrous anthem.
O mysterious Slavic soul,
O vodka!

All efforts are rehearsed:
chorus without orchestra,
orchestra without chorus,
chorus with orchestra.

Our wonder doesn't win.
They should try it underwater
but no one thinks of that,

underwater music, cod-music,
gurgling away to itself, and bursting
in little bilious bubbles:

Mosfilm director Chiaureli, my great fan,
can't tell a bassoon from a clarinet,
or a piano from a toilet bowl.
Let them shove the bastard's head in it.

Beria, who personally cut up corpses
and flushed them down the toilet,
now wants people to believe he has grown wings.

Our Leader and Teacher makes us crap in our pants.
Instead of selling their souls on credit,
they should let their souls go about without pants.
So much for my creative diarrhoea.

Everyone's up to something.
Some are up to their knees in blood,
some are up to their balls in blood,
some are up to their necks in blood.

Tell Trotsky music that is *arrogant, immature,*
sounds better than ripe flattering flatulence.

The strong- and simple-hearted,
the Mandelstams of this world,
are born for the next. I'm for this.

When at immense expense Gagarin won the space race
and sang 'spontaneously' up there in Vostok One
The Motherland Hears (my apotheosis of the major triad),
old women had to walk a kilometre to fetch water
from freezing wells and lug it all the way back.

The Frog puffs himself up to an Ox,
and we all butter the Ox.

Ah the New Year, the New Year!
Let's drink to this –
that things don't get any better.

Never speak ill of the dead?
I say dig them up
so that I can spit on their faces.

Man is not alone,
someone is always watching,
and if you think that's odd,
or God, you're wrong.

Do not hum to yourself,
you might be overheard.

When they got me out of Leningrad under siege,
sewing machine in one hand, potty in the other,
was it to make me finish my Seventh
to blast at the Nazis across no-man's-land,
or to stop me seeing comrades eat
their pets, then rats, then one another?

◆◆

The production of souls
is more important than the production of tanks.

I don't stick my nose into theoretical discussion.
I leave that to Withered Arm,
who was not, I take it, crushed by a tank.

Critics talk about beauty grace etcetera
but you won't catch me with that bait.

You can sugar-coat a frog
but I still won't put it in my mouth.

We know what the likes of Zhdanov do
in the name of high art; but silence,
silence is all that music murders.

Don't give me noble aims,
engineers of the human soul etcetera.

Has my music engineered a soul?
Has my soul been engineered?
I don't know, I don't want to know.

Are people marching to the promised land
singing my songs with a gun at their back?

Let the soul take care of itself.
Eternity's a bore, a non-starter.

Light-bulbs aren't eternal,
why should music be?
Who wants an eternal light-bulb?

Who wants an eternal me, generation
after generation humming the same old tunes?

And don't think of the dead,
the dead are past it, everlastingly.

♦♦

The Nose: *an anarchist's hand bomb.*
So be it.

Without a nose you're not a man
but without you a nose can become a man.

Right now there are noses walking around
sniffing and becoming important persons.

There are famous artists who do not exist
and musicians who have never played a note.

A non-existent man turns into an existent one
and an existent one suddenly is not.

Do I exist?

There were combs called Meyerhold,
then the man disappeared.

The silence was deathly,
what to do with the combs?

Are they already selling Shostakovich combs?
Are they blowing my tunes on them?

A man turns into nothing
and nothings become important,

then nothing is important.

◆◆

One day a sparrow flew into my dacha
and shat on my unplayed score.

If a sparrow dirties your creative work with his,
that's no great matter. Much worse
is when it is done by personalities
more significant than the sparrow.

Voices of the disappeared, voices of the dead,
their strangled cries tie my guts in knots.
They bear no witness except to the ghost brain,
their small noise echoing amongst my bombast.

They watched our Leader's face for clues,
then shat in their pants with a great load.
The lucky were taken out, wiped down,
brought back. The unlucky were taken out.

The Sublime Doodler made us do that.
The bigger the grimace the greater the load.
Imagine it tipping the scales
against those weightless souls

who could not stomach the smell, who sank
up to their necks in it. But I,
I contained myself, I tell you.
That is what you are to believe.

I rave like this to not go mad,
to suffer the ordure, to not stink, to not be
one of those who ever stank, or sank.

◆◆

We are the masterpiece makers.
Freshly baked odes to the great and the wise:
it'll be hot but I can't vouch for the taste.

We're all replaceable. Behind your back
feel your replacement ready to screw you, numerous
nameless nobodies waiting for the signal to sit at your desk
and write your novel, your symphony, your poem.

The Master of Harmony calls us all screws
in his miraculous machine, his harmonious
euphonium, his euphonious harmonium.

Red Beethovens spring up out of the blue.
One screw does for another just like that:
from today you'll be a genius screw,

and so you are. Anybody can become a hero here.
Gogol's *extraordinary nimbleness of thought*:
Excellency, give the order and I'll switch over presto.

Any day a bright new screw, a shiny Shostakovich,
could appear and I disappear. Yesterday you were the best,
today you're nobody. Zero. Zilch. Screwed.

Change your address, maybe they'll leave you alone.
Ghost composers people the provinces,
musical slaves in the sticks writing sweets from shit.

Life is getting better, life is getting merrier,
sang the Wise Father,
then in some remote spot had the lot shot.

Some days I wonder if it has not
happened already, if I am really here,
if I have not disappeared,

and who speaks to you now is not a figment,
his song sung and story over.

I've screwed the pitch so high
something has snapped, I've snapped.

When is a figment not a figment?
When it's a figment.

♦♦

The sky is dressed in a gendarme's blue-grey trousers.

He stares at me from my desk: I bin a symphony.
The world of sound is limitless, but brains are limited.

Great chunks of the man's life missing, Mussorgsky,

who brought bent backs and trampled lives
into our music, who dodged the sleuths of history,

one of those dolls you can't knock down,
idiot lying low to bob up again and again,

agreed with you as far as the door.
Then carried on.

◆◆

I am possessed, the Boss's pet.
I hunker down, I grin, I grit my teeth,
I answer different people differently,
I answer the same people differently.

I can do you sad, I can do you happy,
I can do you saccharine
till it sets your teeth on edge,
I can do you fake, I can do you anything

except the full-throated thing,
outpourings from the heart and so on:
it turns sour, the balkanised brain
goes into manic ironic mode.

But I can't do you.
I leave that to the Great Guide,
who never forgets, not anyone.
He'll sniff us all out in the end.

Can the Dog smell his own breath then?

♦♦

The Morning Greets Us with Coolness.
That song saved my life they say.
But was it worth it?
To return from the dead is easy.

It means pretending you never lived,
that your wits are about you and the notes
that come unbidden from the stewed brain
are original and tuneful and of the rollicking sort
which Club Foot and his folk all want to dance to
and that their voice sings through you
like some mighty purgative, *Our bright belief*
is strong, our happiness forever – forward, forward,
forward to an utterly brand new land,
a clean white tabula rasa where we all
plant crops and start new settlements
with wheat fields rippling like sea waves
and lovely neighbours coping and children
spiralling in happy formation in a maze
between campsites, until majestic cities
rise up, rise up, glittering and winking
to each other across the generations.

Easy, did I say? It is exhausting.

♦♦

Composers must master one instrument at least,
piano, piccolo, it doesn't matter.
Even the triangle.
Surely the Ox can manage the triangle.

Look at him there in the back row
fixing the conductor with gimlet eyes
counting the rests – plenty of rests
for the glinty triangle.

When the Great Ox rests
you know he's up to no good,
writing edicts in his head
about the historical necessity
to do for discord

with the help of a purge or two if need be.
The Ox's trill. His thrill.

♦♦

One-ski, two-ski, three-ski:

We spy an anti-person artist,
non-realistic, formalistic.

Music, music,
it must be definitely authentic,
it must be absolutely authentic,
it simply has to be authentic,
it must be definitely gorgeous,
it must be absolutely gorgeous,
it simply must be gorgeous.

It must be optimistic,
it must be realistic,
optimistic, realistic,
realistic, optimistic
– not the naturalistic
noise of a road drill
or musical gas-chamber,

and not, decidedly not
music futuristic, ironistic,
pessimistic, modernistic.
For that is death all round,
and all-round death stinks.

Light music with a vengeance,
the heaviest light you'll ever hear,

cod for the Ox to swallow.

♦♦

Devils, enemies of the people:

cows moo, dogs howl and moan, horses neigh.
Does the enemy of the people admit that…?
The cow is silent. They stick a spear in its side.
The cow moos. *Guilty, it admits it is guilty.*

Silence is a sign of guilt, so is mooing.
Bonfires. Overheated executioners.
Which is the beast, which the man?

Art aspires to the condition of music.
Music aspires to the condition of silence.
Silence aspires to the condition of death.

So art is death. It is very simple:
if our Leader doesn't write music
or books, or paint, but cuts people up,
his art is butchery.

That thought keeps your trap shut
– or opens it in whispers,
in bars, at street corners:

you die today, and I'll die tomorrow.
It is beautifully symmetrical.
It is called being a patron of the arts.

Feel the wheels turn,

watch ex-prisoner and informer
bow to each other across the foyer,

see the silhouettes appear
and disappear along the corridor.

♦♦

We live in the dark
and I'm learning to see in the dark.

Up with mediocrity.
Up yours my music says.
I am not mediocre:
I wear thick specs.

I stare at Tchaikovsky
and he stares back.

The Boss is on the phone
letting his henchman
have it: don't complain
to Stalin about Stalin.
One bully does for another.

Out of politeness I turn away.
The classic and I study each other.
Suddenly I am dismissed
to a brand new life.

Ever since that day
I can reproduce Pyotr Ilyich's beard,
every hair and fleck of it.

As for the dark,
I can see as far as the next man,

which is not very far
to judge from the number
who disappear into it.

♦♦

Death is simple, after all
(stabbing through the eyes for instance,
or nails pounded into the skull
in regular staccato over and over).

If a person's to die, he'll die anyway,
if a person's to live, he'll live anyway,

but I prefer to tiptoe,
a grotesque elephant dance.

In his dacha Club Foot
twitches an eyebrow,
and that's it, you're done for,
the little runt is dead.

I lead a charmed life: I live.

Some charm, some life.

♦♦

You are hungry,
I cook an omelette,
you eat the omelette,

but he, he talks
about the omelette,
he delivers a discourse
on the essence of omelette.

My music says it all
without historical or hysterical
commentary from luminaries,
curly-haired or bald,
bearded or clean-shaven.

Humanists, teachers, thinkers,
musicologists, stuff the lot of them.
I write for the people,
angels, victims, zealots, crooks,
thugs, losers, apparatchiks even.

Love us when we're dirty,
anyone will love us when we're clean,
but even that's a moot point.
Everyone will love us when we're dead.

Don't try to save humanity
in one fell swoop. The Great Doctor
had a go at that, and look who's left.

The others have all been saved
somewhere to the back of beyond,
some beyond that,

and then there's me
hanging on to celebrate
with the art of anticlimax,
my slow diminuendo.

♦♦

Best not write anything big on days
when the Wolf is out and about
with his ear-trumpet and sniffer dogs,

just quiet things, string quartets,
nook-and-cranny music,
music for the drawer.

Sometimes I think I'd like to live
in the crannies, in the back of beyond.

Probably not, probably not…

What I tell you is that I have nothing to tell you.
What I say is that I have nothing to say.
That is what my music says over and over.

★★★

I work myself into the music
and out the other side. What's left
is notes and noise, pure as the driven –

as the snow driven from the Urals,
scurrying and dissolving souls
crowding this cramped flat where I compose

notes of myself and of my draggled
surviving companions,

and Siberia fills with ghosts.

When I remember my friends
all I see is corpses, mountains of corpses.

◆◆

The bigger the lie the more you'll get the point.
Russia is the homeland of elephants.
It all took place in Tsarist Russia.

Truth-tellers live in fear,
conspirators do their stuff in the loo
then flush for authenticity.

My music flushes for authenticity,
it flushes for authority.
It's obvious if you've ears to hear.

I flush for my music,
my music flushes for everybody,
every note I write is a send-up:

my huge C major goes
so over the top you won't believe it
– and you mustn't, ever.

Gigantomania unheard before,
I disappear into it,
vanish in the flash of a baton.

Now you hear me now you don't.

♦♦

Thank you, everything is fine.
Our great Josif Vissarionovich,
ruler of half the world, rings me up,
little me, a worm, a mere worm
compared with His Excellency.

(Nina laughs: not to her I'm not,
but a stubborn curmudgeon,
who meets his deadlines
and lets life go to hell
and domestic pandemonium.)

Dashed it off in a night.
They shook me by the hand and paid me,
paid for my *Song of the Forests*.
It was infused with the zeal
of Soviet etcetera etcetera

– with vodka more like. I sobbed,
I buried my head in the pillow:
vacuity of the void,
profoundly harmonious drivel,
harmony of the fatuous spheres,
my mighty funk.

How to climb into history on all fours,
how to sniff the grand posterior,
that mighty arse,
without getting it up your nose,
in this USSR of ours,
this land of ersatz palaces,

like Nalbandian's delirious dacha,
cornucopia of cupolas,
St Saviour-on-the-Moustache:
payment for squirming,
for buttering the Ox,

or at any rate not getting shot,
though he must have shat himself
when called to the Kremlin
to paint our Leader and Teacher for all time.

Taking the worm's eye view
he did Roach Whiskers from below
– who looms, the little man with the withered arm,
with club-foot and midget bum, looms,
the Gangster, the Man of Steel,
the Compassionate One,
bristles and looms.

We are all worms tunnelling
the gutted eviscerate soil.

◆◆

I'm no Pasternak, no pig kicked
out of the kitchen garden. I did my bit,
I grovelled in New York for the Boss
and wondered how much longer I had to live.

Shostakovich buys his drugs in this store.
Hey, Shosti, do you prefer blondes or brunettes?
Come on, Shosti, jump like Kasyankina.

I shafted Stravinsky, his *nihilistic writings*,
in a speech I did not write; I confessed my sins
in boilerplate answers to malicious questions,
mumbo-jumbo for the Grand Panjandrum.

Lickspittle is the order of the day.
I promise something with a killing title
so they don't stone me or string me up.
Then I forget it and hope they do too:

The Quiet Don will stay that way,
The Cement Sets will never set,
don't ask about *How the Steel*
Was Tempered or I get heated.

The slavery of ideas: that revolting
peace dove by Picasso, how I hate it.
He can say what he likes, I can't.

◆◆

Look at that smile,
the smile of a condemned man,
that snapped rictus grin.

I want to strangle someone, anyone.
Instead I keep my hands to myself,
I sit on them, hands under arse.

That way I can't sign anything.
Signers get shafted, like everyone else,
only with more finesse.

I smile with one half of me,
one half of my face: a stroke,
a stroke of genius.

◆◆

Dim-witted workers of the 'punitive organs'
in the Finnish house next to our dacha
chuck litter and insults over the fence.

They know an enemy of the people
when they hear one: I work at the piano
trying to fabricate my formalist rubbish.

But day in day out
their loudspeaker propaganda
stuns the brain. No music comes.

In our tree-house a catapult twangs: silence,
sweet silence! Young Maxim grins, imagines:
a Finnish sniper, a Soviet soldier dead.

The rush of a shied stone enters my head:
a catgut plucked – then a string quartet
stirs snow-bound silences, White Death.

◆◆

Scotch the formalist snake.

From now until forever:
refined, harmonious, melodious.

Do not touch this cloud-dweller
said the Kremlin Caligula.
I'm no cloud-dweller, no Pasternak,
so what saved my neck?

Hear me chase my tail
in censor-dodging circles.

It's drivel, not art.
Artful drivel, devil's drivel,
twisting on the Ox's hot spit.

You must not take me at my word,
you must take me at my lack of word,
you must take me at my music.

If you want to keep a secret
you must keep it to yourself,
you must keep it from yourself.
If you want to keep a secret
you must have no secret.

The verbiage will fade,
but with music what you hear
is what you get: you get me.

You must hear me out,
you must see me through,
you must see through me.

Our Mighty Maestro
doesn't like the minor,

it isn't happy, isn't carefree.
So I've done some frantic major.
(They quantify my works by key.)

Not the notes
but what's between
– I like the sound of that: I live
between, I live among, I live in
my music, I just about live.

All the rest passes for life.
Go with how it sounds
and forget the rest.

There is no rest, all I have
is restlessness. Give me rest,
bars and bars of it

for the long drop
into the self.
His only real life was his art,
and into it he admitted no one.

Yes, that's it. Get carving.

♦♦

God walked in the Garden of Eden,

Stalin walks in the garden of the Kremlin
reciting poetry and tending trees,

and Dmitri Dmitriyevich Shostakovich
writes the music to save his skin.

There are only three kinds of hero now,
the dead, the maimed, and Stalin.

I say there's a fourth: the music man.

★★★

For some reason everyone speaks quietly.
Every toady expects a miracle.
Stalin will give birth.

They agree, carefully and quietly,
today the Great Gardener will give birth,
the man with the mighty moustache
and the withered arm will give birth.

This music is not melodious,
not aesthetical, not harmonious.

The composer bids farewell to his score,
to his career, perhaps to something more.

◆◆

What a disgusting
unmusical thing
coloratura is.

Fascinating
the states of non-being.
Dematerialisation,

now there's a word.
Dematerialisation
is not liquidation.

He accomplishes
his dematerialisation
and is not heard of again.

One day he is there, the next he is not.
No one says a word, your name
vanishes from the conversation, that is all.

Of you we must not say you never were,
of you we must not say anything,
of you we must not remember anything,
there must be nothing to remember.

He is not dead for he was not alive.
He is not and was not,
remember – or rather forget,

that he ever was,
if he ever was…

You see, already it is happening,
the havering, the forgetting, although

he can reappear,
in a queue, at a corner,

hovering, whom you
must nevertheless

remember to forget – or just
forget. The mind
goes round in mad loops.

But, to be dead
is to have been,
and be no longer.

To be dead
is not being.
He was,
but he is not.

You do not volunteer
to disappear, you just
disappear, you are
liquidated, you evaporate.

But the result is the same,
you are not heard of again.

All pray that the next
will be somebody else.
It usually is.

Everyone thinks I am next,
tomorrow Dmitri Dmitriyevich
Shostakovich will disappear.

I would rather be dead, people say,
but that is a self-fulfilling prophecy.
I said *I envy him his death*, but did I?

Has my whole life been
displacement activity
on a grand scale?

Playing dead is what I do best.

Is real death music then?
I come to life in it,
I die into it, I am it,
I speak to you from it:

listen to me it says,
I give nothing away,
I am elsewhere,
in a chant, a crazy
defiant chant,

a grim spirit,
a ghastly ghost,
a ghostly gasp.

Death has been done to death.

The riff is ended

morendo

morendo

♦♦

Do not contemplate the navel of art.

There are days when those who love music
make me puke, and there are days
when those who don't do too.

Today I think it is good,
the noise I make,
tomorrow I won't be so sure,

tomorrow I shall play it over
and the notes will sound false,
as grating and grinding

and hollow as I feel
when enduring the sneers
of those who set themselves up,

who conspire and connive
with their snivelling companions
in our great wake,

and someone who calls himself me
will be drivelling with the rest of them,
issuing dead statements

from the department
for the dissemination of rot
in this land of the scarcely living.

Anger is bad for art,
you can hear that now.

It signifies only itself.
It should stop, I should stop,
they all say I should stop,

they who have never written a note
worth hooting by the circling owl.

This noise tells me I exist,
everything else says no.

◆◆

Play it so that flies drop dead in mid-air
and the audience start leaving the hall
from sheer boredom.

You play for yourself,
the audience eavesdrops.

Beware the departing guest
more than the seated one.

It is hard to compose
if the audience does not understand.

It is hard to compose if they do.
I write suicide music, and pray
they just stay schtum.

Call it paranoia,
delusions of grandeur,
grandiosomania,

or simply wanting to disappear
into my own noise.

The bigger the audience
the more the sneaks and snakes.
Everyone is alone.
They sit there and pray to be elsewhere,

or perhaps they are:
the perfect audience
is one, or none.

(I play best to myself.
I do counterpoint
which is against the law.
I keep it in my bottom drawer.)

They said of my Fifth
an audience hand-picked
one by one, a fake success.

We wait for the body count.
Those who survive are stupid,
that is why they survive.

(I have survived so far,
I write music to order,
no more thought
is my prayer.)

Or they pretend,
pretend to be stupid,
faces turning to masks:

what does it mean,
what do you mean?

Mean? It depends what you hear,
it depends what you want to hear,
it depends what they want you to hear,
it depends what I want you not to hear.

The orchestra plays my music,
the cat plays with the mouse,
the Ox plays with us all.

I just play.

◆◆

The Steel Man sings.

He has a fine voice, they say.
It is high tenor.
He was a seminary man, he sang there.

Let him float
up into space with a song,
the Man from Georgia in the stratosphere

where God is near
for a good chin-wag and the odd prayer,
and the devil to croon in his ear.

You should have been a priest
his mother said, they swear.

We all swear down here.

◆◆

Sergei Prokofiev is dead
hung in the air
like an impossibility.

Prokofiev, one of my deaf spots.
So, is the weather here always like this?

No one should dare to die
on the same day as Stalin,
but Sergei beat the Wolf to it
by fifty minutes.

I wasn't there to wave them off
into versts of Elysian field
where thin ghosts flock and jostle
to hear the Five-Year Plans,
the forevers and foralways,
of our club-footed orator Wolf.

No wreaths for Sergei,
the Wolf had snaffled the lot,
while soul upon soul choked to death
in the crush for peeks at the corpse.

I might risk now a musical portrait
of the Kremlin Mountaineer,
not my old thunder, sonic diarrhoea,
writhings and roilings, overwritten
to stifle terror and drown out thought,

but instead I punch out one last time
D S C H.

Let the Wolf howl.
After him, mere mortals.

◆◆

Art is arrogant, it takes no hostages.
But tyrants take them.
They put you face to face with death
then make you dance to their tune.

Our Leader and Teacher,
his tunes were tripe,
they made my ears vomit:
delirium of the Grand Panjandrum.

I danced to my own tune,
I danced the conundrum:
formalistic, ironistic, modernistic,
I rankled, I got under the Ox's skin,

and he got under the bed by proxy
of every living soul from here to Sakhalin,
and of the half-dead and the dying
and the completely dead for all I know.

Whether he died in his bed or under it
I don't know and I don't care. Mad or sane
he murdered more than all the mad
monarchs, emperors, tsars, dictators, ever did.

◆◆

The delicious word death, my foot,
tell that to the corpses
grinding their way to whatever place
beckons with open jaws.

Death makes it all happen I suppose,
the music and the paint and the words
that stave off the inevitable,
the deranged Gangster
grinning at our navel-gazing,
this going round in circles, artistic,
unrealistic, formalistic, autistic
solipsistic circles.

All the art in the world,
full-throated or only pretending,
however crafty, shifty, sly,
cannot outwit death.
Death will gnaw our twisting arty entrails,
and declare them delicious.

How good that there is no one left to lose
and one can weep, writes artful,
artless Anna. We weep all right.
But fifty million ghosts remain to be lost
to the Great Ghost's ravening maw.

What can she say?
That she is living in a lunatic asylum,
that we are all crazy,
that the Gangster was mad?
But then no one would hear her again.

◆◆

Art belongs to the people.
And to whom do the people belong?

In the end I am nothing, nearly nothing,
living in my music, letting the scales fall away,
notes taut and straining, hunted, haunted,

– artist alienated from his art, ventriloquist,
or maybe the dummy sitting on his knee.

Or has bitterness got the better of me
and I need silence, we all need silence?

I'll work on it, I'll cancel myself out,
I shall create silence. Fill it with whatever you like

except me, manipulator of musical cliché,
cacophonist, maker of fake protest,
riddling singer of slippery insinuation,

who shoves the bloody heart in your face:
victim yesterday, toady today.

★★★

Was Schoenberg right after all?
If it is art it is not for everybody,
if it is for everybody it is not art.

My art is for everybody, and nobody,
not to be understood by anybody,
even by me, for brains are limited
but the world of sound is not.

Football's an art, and it's for everybody.
I'm a trained referee, I know the rules by heart.
(And a tennis umpire: *Don't argue with the umpire,*
I once said to the head of the KGB.)

But when I've kicked the ball about a bit
my brain is free to write a few bars
of immortal music, or something like.

Imagine razor-head Schoenberg doing that,
settling into twelve-tone after a tackle or two.

My 'profoundly lowbrow' devotion to football...
I root for Zenith, always have, always will:
Leningrad Zenith versus Moscow Locomotives.
Televised matches have nothing on the terraces,

like distilled water and export Stolichnaya...
My head spins, I yell with the crowd,
I bellow with the best. Out of passes, tackles,
feints, shuffles, cross-shots, curls,

an elegant geometry materialises:
an art beyond me, beyond all this, beyond...
art that affirms the ultimate rightness of reality:
was football what Gorky was on about?

Feints and passes: I know how to nick
Schoenberg's atonal when I need it.

The crowd's roar ascends
to the sun's stunned silence.

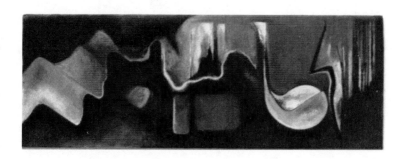

♦♦

Bloody Sunday?
I can do you a Bloody Sunday.
Every Sunday is bloody,
every Sunday throughout history,

some year, some where,
nineteen hundred and blah blah blah,
here, there, bloody everywhere.

All Great Men would penetrate
the cerebral cortex of history,
the Ox butchered the people, my violin-squeals
insinuate themselves into your brain cells.

The dictator's wet dream means blood on the floor.
I pray not to come back to life sometime
spewing harmonious tripe for self-preservation,

belchings of the spheres, gargantua for the masses.

◆◆

Suddenly I am absolved.
The powers that be show mercy
with an extra dose of madness.
I am rehabilitated.

I have been shafted over and over
but now I am to be considered a virgin.

It's simple, so very simple.
I am a person again.
Again I am a person.

An Historical Decree
does for an Historical Decree.

History's a whore,
it lies like an eyewitness.

And please, no posthumous rehabilitation.
Somehow I still don't feel like a virgin.

◆◆

Let us sing a song
gorgeous, realistic, optimistic,
not naturalistic like a road drill
or musical gas-chamber.

Let us raise a glass
to this great historical decree
On Abrogating the Great Historical Decree
that did for Myaskovsky,
poisoned the lives of gifted youth,
promoted trash, and broke Prokofiev

– brutal, inhuman, shameful,
like our anti-abortion law
that murders countless women
reduced to knitting-needles
against children who'll die early.

Yes, I know I parroted
that self-flagellating drivel
concocted by some nobody,
some I-shit-ovsky,
I am an enemy of the people etcetera.

I am a paltry parasite,
a cut-out paper doll on a string.
But I go on writing music,
defeated, ugly, pessimistic,

or, beyond all this,
serene.
        For I remember
imagining contrary things,

I remember hearing
sounds just out of reach.

◆◆

Deputy to the Supreme Soviet,
Artist of the People of the Soviet Union,
Delegate to the Congress for World Peace,
First Secretary of the Russian Composers' Union,

etcetera, and I have the cheek
to tell a young composer
Don't be afraid, be yourself,
take your own incorrect way.

Musical tongue-in-cheek is my way.

Yes-men do tongue-in-cheek,
their tongues in his cheeks,
cheeks of the charmer,
His Mighty Cheeks.

Charmer and snake,
writhing and slithering in his suave pit.

◆◆

Everyone wants to be clean
now that the new dawn has come.

How do you want me to render white silence in music?
I still watch the shadows.

Miraculously, or by leave of the Chosen Ones,
I survive into this age where trust is possible
or so they say. I don't. Too late for that.

The times are new but the informers are old,
the devil is dead but the demon isn't.

I don't trust myself, why trust anybody?
That's my prophylactic against imposture and deceit.

I don't give anything away, notes straining,
strained, stripped, astringent, remote...

memory re-created they call it.
What in hell do I remember, what forget?

Oblivion is the natural lot
of anyone not present.

The dead are served up to posterity,
great men are cut into digestible bits,
the tongue is served separately,
or the nose is a particular delicacy.

I do not forget
what I want to forget, I remember
what I do not want to remember.

What if they've even twisted that
and the things that haunt never happened
except in the head, the myriad brain cells?

– prison cells more like, cells stuffed
with friends, foes, who knows, I don't.

Look me in the eye.
We look past one another,
we see through one another.

Why are your eyes so shifty today?
Why do you look away?
Why do you not look me in the eye?

Look at Himself the wrong way
and you lost your head.

Maybe I lost my head,
everybody knows I've lost face.

We see it all and we know it all
and we say nothing.
We've all turned traitor,

no-eyes, ciphers, paper-pushers,
knifers, condemned to no life,
death's lifers.

Years ago I listened to the noise of time.
It took revenge. Now I want
noise out of time, white silence,
the silence that speaks for itself.

I grow into my inheritance,
I learn this caustic acoustic,
absolute, obdurate, lone.

◆◆

Gagarin sings my song in space.

Mine the first notes ever up there
dwindling beyond the stratosphere

forever while we go on dying
and the unborn turn to dust

to revolve in their eternal
interstellar interludes.

Dwindle dwindle little star
dwindle in the minor

degrow like a jellyfish,
thin to radiant plasma,

echo to lovely nowhere.

Gagarin sings beyond the skies
intergalactic platitudes.

◆◆

I have wept three times,
for my father's death,
for Nina's death,
and for mine.

I dedicate this work to my own memory,
and *to the victims of fascism.* Same thing.

A pseudo-tragedy,
a mishmash of self-quotation,
my tears as plentiful
as the piss from six beers,
ideologically flawed
and of use to nobody.

I've been a whore, I am
and always will be a whore.
I clapped when the others clapped.
They said I was no good
and I clapped.

They powdered my brains.
I wrestled with Marxist-Leninist
musical mysteries.
Are you a materialist or an idealist?
I am a pianist.
It was torture by boredom.
I even went to agitprop car rallies.

The caged bird:
they squeezed me by the throat
and said *now sing,*
and I heard the noise of my own voice:
I am grateful to the Party
for having me.

Words are not my thing, I say.

You can say I played the idiot,
yes-man to a madman, that Russia
is a madhouse so that's all right.
But my noise is music,
it does not speak lickspittle.

Do not interrogate me,
interrogate my music
where I escape into myself
or from myself: I don't know which.

My Fifth ends *me, me, me,*
my Eighth is pseudo-tragic,
my Ninth is pseudo-comic,
my Twelfth is socialist realism
gone mad – or so I like to think.

◆◆

An improvised life, what is that?
Whom to butter up, whom to run down,
here today, gone tomorrow…

An improvised life
circles the dead certainties:

that we whispered under the blanket,
trusting each other out of fear,

that we piled the telephone with cushions,

that I spent all night by the lift,
at the ready with toothbrush and pants,

that the Fifth's forty-minute ovation
stopped them shooting me,

that I'll sign anything to be left alone,
even if they hand it to me upside down,

that I joined the Party to get shot of them,

that tomorrow I'll have fewer friends,
more enemies, and more, many more,
of the enemies who call themselves friend,

that I can still light a campfire with one match
in any wind.

Still the curs are circling,
and the owl circles the ruins of shattered gods.

◆◆

Pyotr Ilyich said *there is no point*
in trying to be anything other
than what I am. What am I? I am
alive. Is there a point to that?

When you are dead there is no point.
Where there is life there is,
if not hope, themes, there are themes,

and there are variations:
despair, for instance, despair
is a good variation:

when a man is in despair
he still believes in something,
he believes he is alive.

Rejoice therefore,
our business is rejoicing,
our business is rejoicing.

Like a back-alley gang
of strutting tearaways
I accelerate and fugue with myself.

Hear my street-bullying bravado,
hear me cringe, hear me sweat,
hear me dance with death:

skeletons in the streets,
skeletons in the trenches
skeletons in the camps,

skeletons in my head.
The variations wind and coil,
but no man can jump his own shadow.

Give me back me, give me me.

◆◆

Genius and villainy are compatible.
Stalin was a villain, was he a genius?
Am I a genius, am I a villain?

Somebody bangs on your door at midnight.
The next day you can't remember,
but there's your signature in the paper.

I'll sign anything, but I won't hold the pen
unless I have to. Was that letter in *Pravda*
denouncing Sakharov signed by me?

I struggle to my feet, I stretch out a hand,
and people give me the cold shoulder.
Of course, they have clarity
and roses growing in their soul.

So rejoice, our job is to rejoice.

Let us now praise an absolute genius
who has invented a miraculous substance.
One teaspoon sprinkled over the planet
will kill all the creatures on earth.

Rejoice therefore, our job is to rejoice.

A genius. There is only one problem:
how to distribute the invention
evenly over the face of the earth.

But rejoice, our job is to rejoice.

The balance of nuclear terror, this man's
first credo, surrendered to his second,
personal responsibility for the future.

He gazed into his navel, and rejoiced.

First he invents the hydrogen bomb
and entrusts it to tyrants,
then he writes snide brochures.

If they did make me denounce
this future famous humanist,
was it really in spite of myself?

And yet I cannot ever
forgive myself.

But no brochure on earth
can balance the bomb.

◆◆

Paranoia is still my fix
to fox the censors.
They ride my blood rapids,
they scuttle among my brain cells.
I do not know how not to be afraid.

I tell myself, let go, don't scratch,
forget, my medium is music,
gut feeling, music from the guts.

Listen to the squeal, absolute,
remote, the thin squeal,
listen to the catgut vibrate,

it slices the soul to flakes
shimmering and shimmying
to a white destiny,

it holds me transfixed,
it cuts through,
it goes beyond.

How many times can the music fade,
how many times die back,
how many times, how many?

To have heard the sly attenuations
pierce and slide, to have felt
the sap fail, is knowledge enough,
is knowledge shrunk to the core.

Wait for the freshet of sound,
the pained noise of the world,
its importunate pother.

◆◆

I have met history coming the other way.
It's all made up,
metahistory of the mighty mind.
Even if it chews you up and spits you out
it doesn't exist,
except as the bits left out,
the bits that don't fit
into the smooth scheme of things,
the fancy fantastical themes
that never end, that outlast us all.
                              I float
into the mind's dazzle and make-believe.

If I return it will be as a rewound ghost
to repeat myself, to play the old tunes.
I shall be out of step
marching with an irresolute flourish
the other way, any way
but that of the fine folk
in their field of silos and shining corn,
their silvery silence,
                              looking up
in reverent amnesia.

♦♦

The grave straightens out the humpbacked.
Unfortunately corpses don't jump out of graves.

A man with no memory is a corpse,
a man with too much is for the chop.

Somewhere between
is where most of us live.

The corpses carry on with their lives.
So many pass by. You must leave them be

for they are me
but somnambulant sans music.

I don't know if I'm happy,
I don't know if I'm sad,
but I make music,

unlike those who feel by rote,
who have been brain-washed
and heart-washed and wrung out.

Is the dance with death any nimbler now?
Fears are dying but are not dead yet,
chants the visionary, revising poet,

but a dying fear is a ghost
gliding to the land of the dead,
a segueing corpse.

Treat with irony what you hold most dear.
Those you love too much perish.

♦♦

I pretend to pen great thoughts,
that way I needn't applaud.

These days I just listen.
Either I like it or I don't,
but I don't shoot a cannon at sparrows.

Music is wordless,
that's why I'm still here,

a shrimp swimming in sauce,
much honoured, little use,

or a walking mummy,
a resurrected pharaoh.

Everyone whispers and stares
waiting for me to go for good,
to disappear into their idea of me.

My idea of me is simple:
there is none, there is no idea.

I write what I write,
I do not have to have a reason,
I do not have a reason.

Absolute uncertainty,
granite incertitude, flinty absence,
call it what you will,
my notes don't come in bottles.

That is why I like the future:
it isn't, it does not exist,
it is a figment as solid
as the earth I stand on.

◆◆

Unlucky in cards,
unlucky in love,
unlucky in profession.

Petit-bourgeois formalistic contractions,
crudity, wildness, merchant lust.

That anti-talisman, hidden under my shirt,
hangs from my neck to this day,
burning with musical still-births.

A pity our Leader left early:
my opera ends with a prison camp.

Playing at things beyond reason,
it could end very badly.

I bowed, I collected my briefcase,
and I went to the station.

Everyone knew I'd be destroyed,
and the anticipation of that
notable event has never left me.

Muddle instead of music,
inside-out music,
inside-out on purpose.

So be it.
My *creative response to just criticism*
(always that killer claptrap) is

I am inside-out

nerves bared to the air.

◆◆

And outside in.
Peel back the mask and there's another mask.

I circle my skull,
the cavernous tomb of my past,
the echoes and lies,

I circle the concert hall,
the blinkers and winkers
elbowing and nudging
to be the first to suck up or shout down,

to prove in a crowd
they were never one of the crowd,
never one of the brass-faced
lackeys and greasy asses.

Memory smoulders,
ready to flare when I'm gone:

do me as the holy fool if that's what you want,
court jester, idiot, simpleton, joker,
just clown will do.

I dissembled, and I re-assembled myself.
And art made tongue-tied by authority,
and folly doctor-like controlling skill.
Pasternak knew all about that.

★★★

But music is abstract,
it gets it better than words.
Music can say what it likes,

and you can hear what you like.
The world of sound is limitless.
But brains are limited.

74

Our Leader the Orator had verbal diarrhoea,
buckets of it, but even he, half-mad,
beast and butcher, knew about music,

knew that it illuminates through and through,
that it's our last hope, beyond words,
our last retreat, our bolt hole.

So he feared and hated it.

◆◆

I lift the receiver
to save another soul.
Oh that'll be Shostakovich
on one of his mercy missions.

Can music attack evil,
can it make us stop and think,
can it cry out?

Your attitude to reality is unhealthy.
We need an all-healing feeling
of the ultimate rightness of reality.
The poet's answer to exalted humbug,
to rebukes for 'excessive bile' and so on, was

unhealthy reality, unhealthy attitude;
when we begin to get angry more,
then we'll be able to love more, love better,
and not just ourselves but our motherland.

And suddenly you could see far to the ends of the earth.

I see the ultimate murderers,
I see mass graves and stacked corpses
returning to mother earth.

The blood of the innocent will rise from the soil, and sing.

Weep, Russian people,
that is the news, not their brazen lies.

And my music has wept,
for you, for me, for all of us, even for them.

It belongs to a nearby future.
He who has ears will hear.

◆◆

Are they taking good care of you,
Dmitri Dmitriyevich? The man smiles.

In whose hands are you leaving me to die?
Have they made me mad?

We make a mess, then pound our chests
and smear tears all over our face;
we howl and howl, but how can howling help?
That's a slave mentality.

And silence is slavery, as I circle my cell,
my skull, as I go round and round
chained to my brain,
my *well-hammered head.*

Once I wanted the freedom to love,
then all I wanted was the freedom to live.

I am writing for my life, they said.
I said: I am writing,
I am alive. That is all.

I said, work, play, get on with it,
there's no other life, there can't be,
the verbiage will fade,
get back to the desk,

to the music, that wordless monologue;
it will last, I tell you, it will even take you
to the heights of eternal resin, we joked,

but it's no joke now.
Now there may be few notes to write
but there's plenty to play.

Yes I did play the clown,

I played it for all it's worth,
I played for life

– and am allowed to breathe. Give thanks,
thanks to the Kremlin gang,

and to my gradual murder.

Devious, expert at lying low,
I've so much control now, have circled
and dodged and weaved so long,

this honoured hero,
who trailed his cap and bells,

who tried not to lie to himself at least,
who knew once how it is to feel,

how love could have been
(Tatyana, Tatyana),

shrinks into his shell,
his musical carapace,

and clams up.

◆◆

Gymnastics for the dying.

They didn't chop off both my hands.
Instead, paralysis in my right,
and training the left to copy out
Masha eats kasha over and over.

(Composing by tape recorder
is a special taste,
like licking rubber boots.
Prokofiev liked doing that
to orchestrate.)

Without 'Party guidance'
I would have composed
more pure music,
left-handed music,
ideologically flawed
and of use to nobody…

This is how I end,
how I have ended,
how I have ended up,

still struggling for clarity,
still stringing meaningless
notes on lines of air:

having nothing to do
with anything, they are
all I have.
Prithee Nuncle,
shall I live, shall this music live?

♦♦

Today I would make silence.

Silence is forbidden in St Leningrad.
On the streets of that city
there is noise of joy perpetually.

But silence would get inside me,
nuzzling and groping for entry.

Father, what if they hang you for this?

Don't worry, they'll make a fake,
a replacement with knobs on.

How many notes does it take to die?
How many notes does it take to return?

No chorus, no soloist, no apotheosis,
just music, where you will find me
ducking and weaving.

I like it so that no one can hear
except what they choose.

What's it about?

What's it ever about?
Work it out for yourself,
make what you will of me.

You won't know what I thought,
you won't know what I felt,

I do not know myself
though I thought and felt enough.

I am not here,
nail down the lid,
throw in the earth.

It trickles still.

Notes

p. 4, 'Listen, I give you sound'
This poem ends with the memory of an incident Shostakovich is supposed to have witnessed during the October Revolution of 1917, when he was eleven.

p. 7, 'The future, it will blow over'
In later years Solzhenitsyn thought Shostakovich was a stooge and Shostakovich thought Solzhenitsyn was messianic.

p. 8, '*Muddle Instead of Music*'
The first line is the title of an infamous 1936 *Pravda* editorial (certainly sanctioned by Stalin, even if he did not write it) condemning Shostakovich's highly successful opera *Lady Macbeth of the Mtsensk District*. 'Crucified on the staves' quotes Yevtushenko on the twenty-six-year suppression of the opera. The opera's heroine is Katerina Izmailova. Shostakovich's first wife was Nina Varzar.

p. 12, 'The circus is pure art'
In the sequence Stalin is called by several names, most frequently 'the Ox' (also 'Lover of Euphony', 'Grand Panjandrum', 'Leader and Teacher', 'Master of Harmony', 'Wise Father', 'the Boss', 'the Great Guide', 'Great Doctor', 'the Wolf', 'the Kremlin Caligula', 'Mighty Maestro', 'the Great Gardener', 'the Steel Man', 'the Gangster', etc.).

p. 13, 'Hamlet farts through a flute'
Shostakovich wrote the music for Nikolai Akimov's irreverent 1932 production of *Hamlet*, in which the prince dramatises his contempt for Rosencrantz and Guildenstern, who try to play him like a pipe, by lowering a flute to his buttocks while a piccolo pipes out Alexander Davidenko's mass song 'They Wanted to Beat Us, to Beat Us'.

p. 14, 'No toadstools?'
'The Big House': the headquarters of the Leningrad NKVD (1937; later the KGB). 'The monkey's ominous cry': a reference to one of

Shostakovich's favourite compositions, Mahler's *Das Lied von der Erde*.

p. 16, '*An anthem, do me an anthem*'
Lavrenti Beria was the head of Stalin's secret police apparatus. '*Instead of selling ... without pants*': lines by the satirical poet Sasha Chyorny (Alexander Glikberg). While orbiting the earth the Soviet cosmonaut Yuri Gagarin sang the song 'The Motherland Hears' set to music by Shostakovich. 'Apotheosis of the major triad': Khachaturian's description of the setting.

p. 19, '*The production of souls*'
The first two lines were said by Stalin, who had a withered arm. Andrei Zhdanov, a major perpetrator of the Soviet Union's Great Purge in the 1930s, became director of the Union's cultural policy after World War II and leader of the 'anti-formalism' campaign against prominent Soviet composers.

p. 20, '*The Nose: an anarchist's hand bomb*'
This poem refers to Shostakovich's opera *The Nose*, which is based on the satirical short story of that name by Gogol.

p. 21, 'One day a sparrow flew into my dacha'
Composers were known to behave as described here when Stalin (a keen doodler) was 'auditing' their work.

p. 24, '*The sky is dressed in a gendarme's blue-grey trousers*'
The first and third lines quote phrases that appealed to Shostakovich from Mussorgsky's letters.

p. 26, '*The Morning Greets Us with Coolness*'
Stalin had a club foot.

p. 28, 'One-ski, two-ski, three-ski'
The italicised lines are a rendering of part of Shostakovich's scathing lampoon *Rayok*, satirising the vacuous officialese of the 1948 'Zhdanov' Decree condemning 'formalism' in music. Probably written nine years after the decree (and originally performed only for family and close friends), it is in the style of the popular entertainment 'peepshow' at travelling fairs. 'One-ski' etc. are

cultural apparatchiks (including Zhdanov, who also condemned 'naturalistic noise' in music).

p. 30, 'We live in the dark'
One of the periodic bans on Shostakovich's music was suddenly lifted (in this instance to enable him to write film music, one of Stalin's priorities).

p. 35, '*Thank you, everything is fine*'
Dmitri Nalbandian was one of the most prolific, and sycophantic, of Soviet artists.

p. 37, 'I'm no Pasternak, no pig kicked'
Shostakovich was a member of the Soviet delegation to the Congress for World Peace, New York, 1949. '*Jump like Kasyankina*': Americans shouted this out to Shostakovich on his arrival in New York; Oksana Kasyankina, a Russian teacher at the Soviet Delegation School, had defected by jumping out of an embassy window.

p. 39, 'Dim-witted workers of the "punitive organs"'
The setting is Shostakovich's dacha near the Finnish border in 1948, when he was in public disgrace. The poem refers to the highly effective Finnish sniper, Simo Häyhä, nicknamed 'White Death' by the Red Army during the Russo–Finnish war of 1939–40. 'Maxim' is Shostakovich's son.

p. 40, 'Scotch the formalist snake'
'*His only real life … admitted no one*': diva Galina Vishnevskaya wrote this about Shostakovich.

p. 42, 'God walked in the Garden of Eden'
Shostakovich wrote the music to the 1950 propaganda film *The Fall of Berlin*, an early scene of which is set in Stalin's garden.

p. 48, '*Play it so that flies drop dead in mid-air*'
The first three lines are Shostakovich's instructions to the string quartet playing his Fifteenth (and final) Quartet. '*You play for yourself … eavesdrops*': cellist Mstislav Rostropovich said this.

p. 50, 'The Steel Man sings'
The Steel Man is Stalin.

p. 51, '*Sergei Prokofiev is dead*'
This poem plays on the fact that some have conjectured that the wolf in Prokofiev's *Peter and the Wolf* is Stalin. '*So, is the weather here always like this?*': Shostakovich's response to Prokofiev's description of his creative plans for his Sixth Symphony. 'The Kremlin Mountaineer': Osip Mandelstam's name for Stalin in his 'Stalin Epigram'. 'One last time': the last movement of Shostakovich's Tenth Symphony. 'D S C H': Shostakovich's musical signature motif (the notes D, E flat, C, B, which in German notation spell out D, S, C, H, or Dmitri SCHostakowitsch).

p. 53, 'The delicious word death, my foot'
The first line quotes Whitman. 'Anna' is Anna Akhmatova.

p. 54, '*Art belongs to the people*'
The first line is a statement by Lenin. 'Stolichnaya': superior vodka.

p. 56, 'Bloody Sunday?'
'Bloody Sunday' in Soviet history refers to the massacre of peaceful demonstrators on their approach to the Winter Palace in St Petersburg, the incident that sparked the 1905 Russian Revolution. It is commemorated in Shostakovich's Eleventh Symphony, 'The Year 1905', though many also heard in this symphony rage and despair at contemporary violence and evil.

p. 57, 'Suddenly I am absolved'
'An Historical Decree / does for an Historical Decree': a 1958 Communist Party resolution corrected the 'errors' of the 1948 'Zhdanov' Decree condemning 'formalism'.

p. 59, 'Deputy to the Supreme Soviet'
The 'young composer' is Sofia Gubaidulina.

p. 62, 'Gagarin sings my song in space'
For the background to this poem see the note above for the poem '*An anthem, do me an anthem*'.

p. 63, 'I have wept three times'
'I dedicate this work to my own memory, / and *to the victims of fascism'*: Shostakovich's private and public dedications to his Eighth Quartet. 'A pseudo-tragedy … use to nobody': see Shostakovich's description of his Eighth Quartet in a letter to his friend Isaak Glikman. *'I am grateful to the Party / for having me'*: Shostakovich joined the Communist Party under duress in 1960.

p. 65, 'An improvised life, what is that?'
'And the owl circles the ruins of shattered gods': adapted from a line from Sasha Chyorny's 'Our Posterity', which Shostakovich set to music.

p. 67, *'Genius and villainy are compatible'*
Shostakovich's name appeared as a signatory to a letter in *Pravda* in 1973 denouncing the dissident nuclear physicist Andrei Sakharov. The first line quotes a statement in an 'open letter' by the Soviet writer and human rights activist Lydia Chukovskaya in defence of Sakharov and condemning Shostakovich.

p. 71, *'The grave straightens out the humpbacked'*
The first line is a Russian saying. The 'visionary, revising poet' is Yevtushenko.

p. 74, 'And outside in'
'And art made tongue-tied … Pasternak knew all about that': Shostakovich set to music Pasternak's translation of Shakespeare's Sonnet 66.

p. 76, 'I lift the receiver'
'The poet's answer to exalted humbug': the poet is Nikolay Nekrasov. *'And suddenly you could see…'*: Gogol.

p. 77, *'Are they taking good care of you'*
'Well-hammered head': another phrase that appealed to Shostakovich from Mussorgsky's letters. Shostakovich's first love was Tatyana Glivenko.

p. 79, 'Gymnastics for the dying'
'Paralysis': Shostakovich suffered from a rare form of polio, which

had very debilitating effects in his later years.

p. 80, 'Today I would make silence'
'St Leningrad': Shostakovich's wry joke. 'Father, what if they hang you for this?': reported to be Maxim Shostakovich's whispered remark to his father at a rehearsal of the Eleventh Symphony.

Further Reading

Of the many books about Shostakovich, the following in particular have provided me with a wealth of information. They have also made me appreciate how his life and music can stimulate an extraordinary range of opinion and critical reaction.

Ardov, Revd. Michael, *Memories of Shostakovich: Interviews with the Composer's Children*, trans. Rosanna Kelly and Michael Meylac (London: Short Books, 2004).

Bartlett, Rosamund (ed.), *Shostakovich in Context* (Oxford: Oxford University Press, 2000).

Behrman, Simon, *Shostakovich: Socialism, Stalin & Symphonies* (London: Redwords, 2010).

Brown, Malcolm Hamrick (ed.), *A Shostakovich Casebook* (Bloomington: Indiana University Press, 2004).

Fay, Laurel E., *Shostakovich: A Life* (New York: Oxford University Press, 2000).

Glikman, Isaak, *Story of a Friendship: The Letters of Dmitry Shostakovich to Isaak Glikman 1941–1975 with a Commentary by Isaak Glikman*, trans. Anthony Phillips (London: Faber, 2001).

Lesser, Wendy, *Music for Silenced Voices: Shostakovich and his Fifteen Quartets* (New Haven: Yale University Press, 2011).

MacDonald, Ian, *The New Shostakovich*, new edn, revised by Raymond Clarke (London: Pimlico, 2006).

Morton, Brian, *Shostakovich: His Life and Music* (London: Haus Books, 2006).

Norris, Christopher, *Shostakovich: The Man and his Music* (London: Lawrence and Wishart, 1982).

Quigley, Sarah, *The Conductor* (Toronto: Harper Collins, 2012).

Ross, Alex, *The Rest is Noise: Listening to the Twentieth Century* (London: Fourth Estate, 2008).

Vishnevskaya, Galina, *Galina: A Russian Story*, trans. Guy Daniels (San Diego: Harcourt, 1984).

Volkov, Solomon, *Shostakovich and Stalin: The Extraordinary Relationship between the Great Composer and the Brutal Dictator*, trans. Antonina W. Bouis (London: Little Brown, 2004).

Volkov, Solomon, *Testimony: The Memoirs of Dmitri Shostakovich as Related to and Edited by Solomon Volkov*, trans. Antonina W.

Bouis (London: Hamish Hamilton, 1979).

Wilson, Elizabeth, *Shostakovich: A Life Remembered*, new edn (London: Faber, 2006).